info Stickers

Sharks

 A world of sharks

 Friends, family, neighbours

 Cutting, biting, tearing

 Weird and wonderful

 Swimming and hunting

 Strange sharks

 Shark food

A world of sharks

Some sharks are bigger than buses; others would fit in
the palm of your hand. Only a few sharks are dangerous to humans.
Most won't harm people unless they feel threatened.

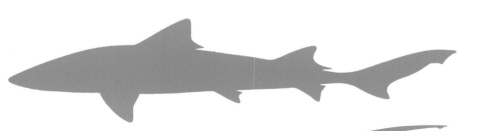

Mako shark's tail
Makos have strong tails that help
them to swim quickly. They can
reach speeds of 35 kmph (22 mph),
and can jump 6 metres
(20 ft) in the air.

Leopard shark
These harmless sharks have large, blotchy markings.
They survive well in captivity, and are often kept in
public aquariums.

Thresher shark's tail
The thresher shark has by far the
longest tail of any shark. It is as
long as the rest of its body.

Tiger shark's tail
The long upper part of its tail
helps this shark to twist and turn
quickly when chasing fast prey.

Bull shark
This is the only shark that can swim in fresh
water. It has been seen 2,800 kilometres
(1,750 mi) up the Mississippi River, and 4,000
kilometres (2,500 mi) up the Amazon River.

Chain catshark
This is one of the groundsharks, the
largest of all the shark families. It is a
small shark with long catlike eyes.

Swellshark
Swellsharks hide in rock crevices
or other narrow places. When
threatened, they swallow water to
swell themselves up. This wedges
them tightly inside their hiding place,
so enemies cannot pull them out.

Megamouth shark
This huge shark was unknown until
1976. Only about 12 of them have
ever been seen. It gets its name
from its huge mouth.

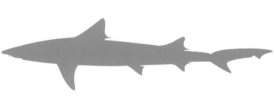

Cookiecutter shark
This small shark is named because it takes bite-sized plugs out of its
prey. It attacks other fish and even dolphins.

Atlantic weasel shark
This brightly striped shark is one of seven
weasel sharks.

Friends and neighbours

Sharks have some close relatives. These include the chimaeras and rays. Many other animals share the shark's watery world and live alongside them, some even getting quite attached.

Spookfish
The spookfish is a chimaera, a relative of sharks. It has a long nose that has taste and touch sensors to help it find food.

Giant squid
No one has ever seen a living giant squid, but dead animals are sometimes washed up on shore. These squids can be up to 18 metres (60 ft) long.

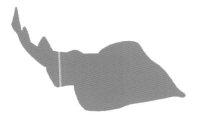

Guitarfish
Some guitarfish are very curious. These rays can even stand up on the tips of their fins to get a good look at a diver.

Scuba diver
Many people enjoy diving where they can see sharks. It is unusual for a shark to bother a diver, as most sharks are not harmful.

Cleaner wrasse
How do sharks clean their teeth? Answer: with fish! These brave little fish swim right inside a shark's mouth and clean its teeth.

Remora
These fish swim up to a shark, find a comfortable spot, and attach themselves to it. They hitchhike to catch any leftovers that a shark drops or misses.

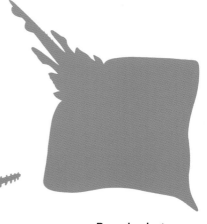

Rough skate
Skates and rays have fins at the sides that help them to move forward. This is unlike their shark relatives, which use their tails to move through the water.

Sea star
Sea stars share shallow waters with many kinds of sharks. They eat shellfish and coral polyps.

Sawfish
Sawfish look like a cross between a shark and a ray. Their long snout is shaped like a toothed sword. They use it to stun the small fish they eat.

Cutting, biting, tearing

Sharks go through thousands of teeth in their lifetime. As old teeth wear out, a new row of teeth behind will replace them. This means they are always sharp. Yet, for all their amazing teeth, sharks cannot chew.

Harlequin tuskfish
Some fish, like this harlequin tuskfish, are swallowed whole by reef sharks. They have to do this because they can't chew at all.

Shortfin mako shark's tooth
Makos have thin, needle-like, stabbing teeth. These help the shark grab prey such as fish that are very fast.

Great white shark
This large, fierce shark has attacked humans, but mostly eats seals and sea lions.

Great white shark's tooth
A great white shark can take a 10-kilogram (22-lb) chunk of flesh from its prey in a single bite! They have huge, triangular, serrated, slicing teeth.

Blue shark's tooth
Blue sharks use their serrated, triangular teeth to feed on large schools of squid. They will also tear into a dead whale or porpoise.

Blue shark
Blue sharks feed mostly at night. Like most large, slender, cigar-shaped sharks, they are graceful swimmers.

Sea urchin
Even the prickly spines of sea urchins do not deter sharks. Horn sharks have special teeth they use to grab and crunch them up.

Shortfin mako shark
As well as their sharp teeth, mako sharks have special jaw muscles that help them catch, hold, and eat their prey easily and quickly.

Horn shark's tooth
These sharks have small, sharp teeth in the front and broad, flat teeth at the back to crush hard shells. Some teeth have small cusps for grabbing soft prey such as squid.

Basking shark
These sharks have very big mouths. They often feed at the surface of the water, close to shore. Despite their huge size, they don't attack humans unless they feel threatened.

Tiger shark's tooth
Tiger sharks are large hunters. Their teeth are sharp and pointed.

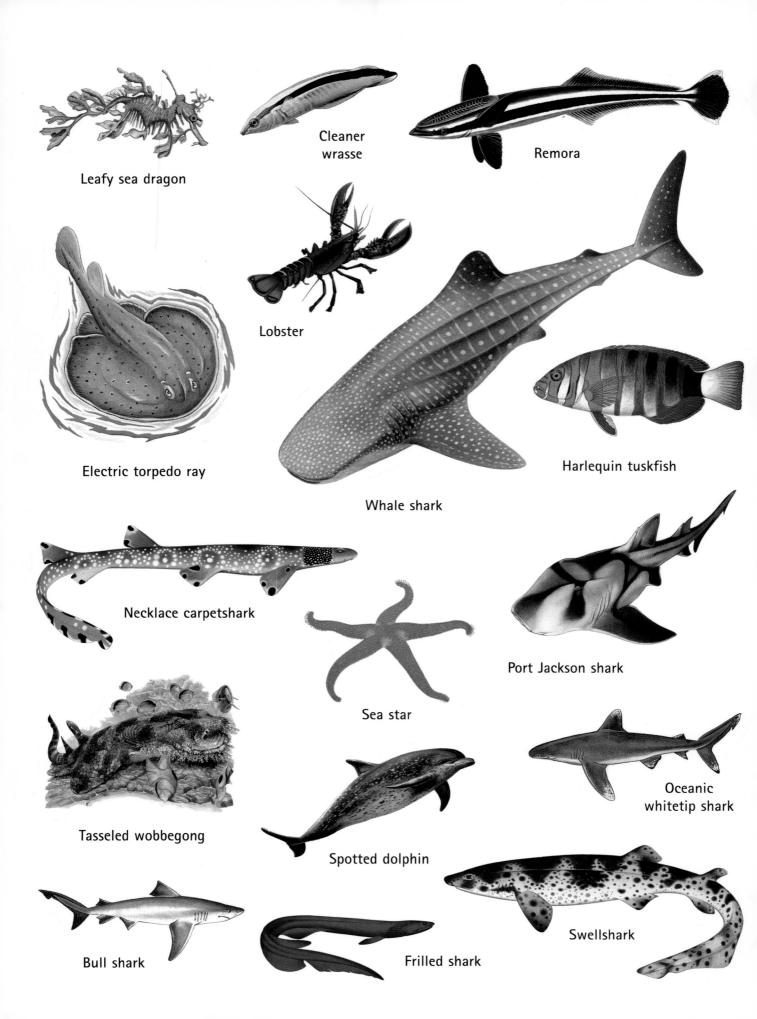

Leafy sea dragon

Cleaner wrasse

Remora

Electric torpedo ray

Lobster

Whale shark

Harlequin tuskfish

Necklace carpetshark

Sea star

Port Jackson shark

Tasseled wobbegong

Spotted dolphin

Oceanic whitetip shark

Bull shark

Frilled shark

Swellshark

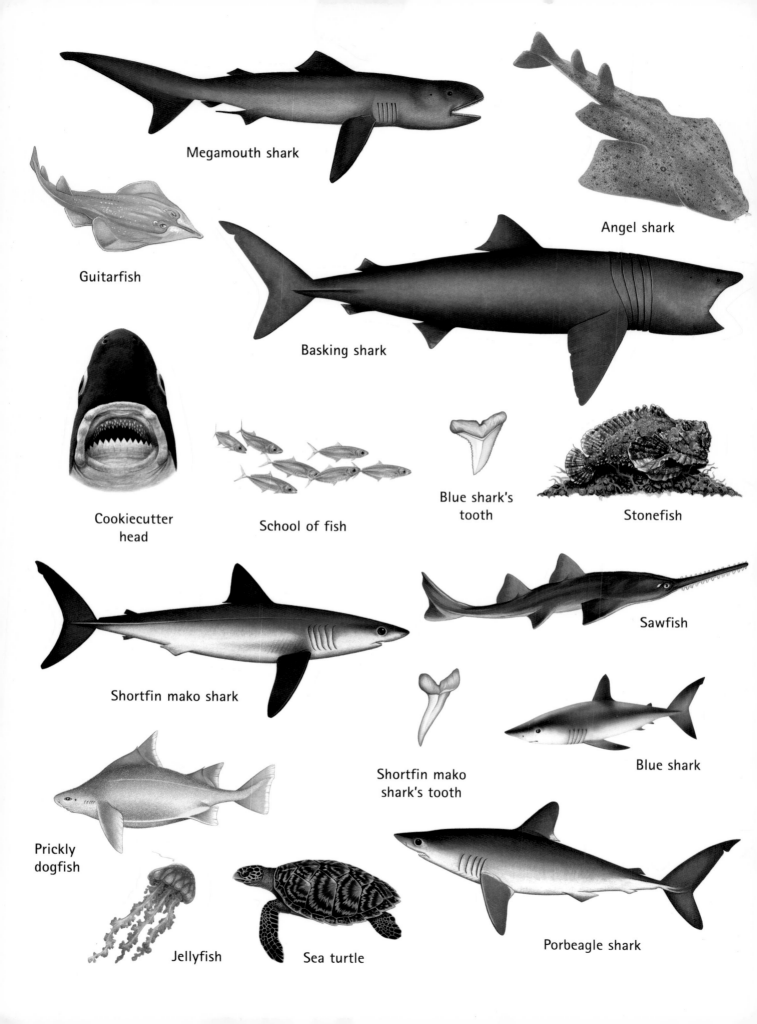

Megamouth shark

Angel shark

Guitarfish

Basking shark

Cookiecutter
head

School of fish

Blue shark's
tooth

Stonefish

Shortfin mako shark

Sawfish

Shortfin mako
shark's tooth

Blue shark

Prickly
dogfish

Jellyfish

Sea turtle

Porbeagle shark

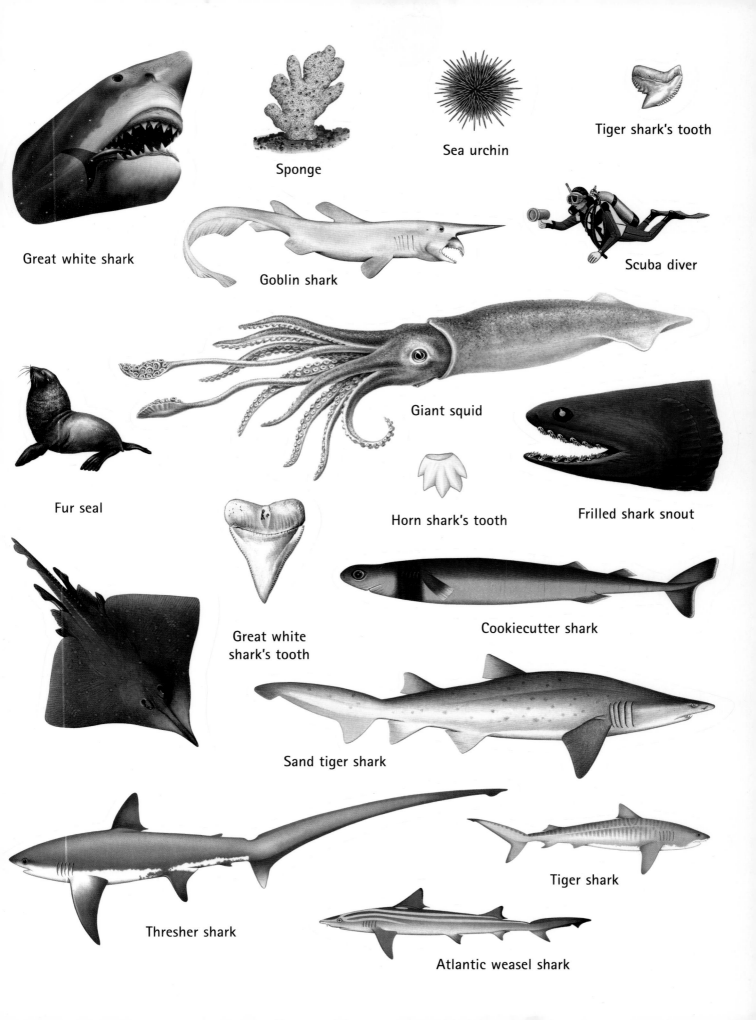

Great white shark

Sponge

Sea urchin

Tiger shark's tooth

Goblin shark

Scuba diver

Giant squid

Fur seal

Horn shark's tooth

Frilled shark snout

Great white shark's tooth

Cookiecutter shark

Sand tiger shark

Thresher shark

Tiger shark

Atlantic weasel shark

Clownfish and
sea anemone

Tiger shark's
tail

Winghead shark's head

Mako shark's tail

Leopard shark

Graceful catshark

Horn shark

Bonnethead
shark's head

Great hammerhead shark

Thresher
shark's tail

Ornate wobbegong

Chain catshark

Scalloped hammerhead

Spookfish

Blacktip reef shark

Shark hatching

Weird and wonderful

Some sharks and other sea animals look odd, or behave in strange ways. Some we know little about because they are seldom seen.

Leafy sea dragon
These fish are related to sea horses. They are disguised to blend in with the seaweed forests where they live.

Clownfish and sea anemone
Clownfish are protected by living among the stinging tentacles of sea anemones.

Jellyfish
Jellyfish float through warm seas. They are related to sea anemones.

Cookiecutter head
Cookiecutters live in the deep water of the ocean. Their jaws and lips act just like a suction cup.

Sponge
Sponges attach themselves to coral reefs and feed on tiny particles that float by.

Scalloped hammerhead
Hammerhead sharks roam the seabed, searching for stingrays to eat. They use their head to pin the stingrays onto the sandy bottom, then they devour them.

Frilled shark
The ruffled edges of its gills give this shark its name. Because it lives in deep waters where humans cannot go, it is seldom seen, and we know very little about it.

Stonefish
Stonefish are disguised to look just like rocks. This is dangerous for waders, because stonefish inject a deadly poison from their spines if they are stepped on.

Electric torpedo ray
In their fins, electric rays have special cells that produce electricity. They can make enough electricity to knock out a human.

Swimming and hunting

Sharks spend a lot of time swimming, hunting, and feeding. They use their fins and large muscles to keep moving through the water, their eyes to see, and their noses to smell.

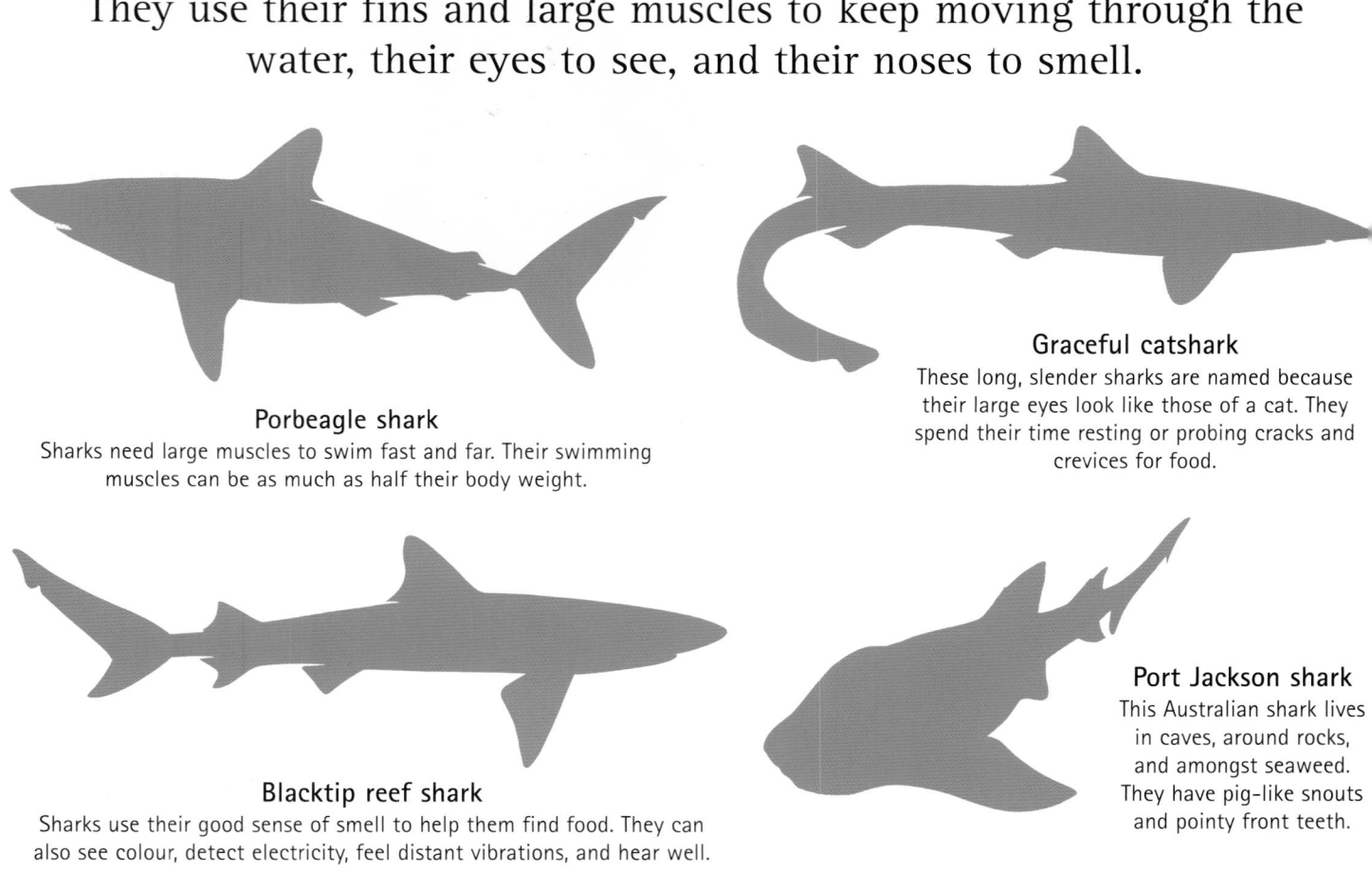

Porbeagle shark
Sharks need large muscles to swim fast and far. Their swimming muscles can be as much as half their body weight.

Graceful catshark
These long, slender sharks are named because their large eyes look like those of a cat. They spend their time resting or probing cracks and crevices for food.

Blacktip reef shark
Sharks use their good sense of smell to help them find food. They can also see colour, detect electricity, feel distant vibrations, and hear well.

Port Jackson shark
This Australian shark lives in caves, around rocks, and amongst seaweed. They have pig-like snouts and pointy front teeth.

Shark hatching
A swellshark pup hatches from the egg case that has protected it. A shark's egg can take up to a year to hatch.

Great hammerhead shark
This shark is easy to identify – it has a thick, broad head in the shape of a hammer or a mallet. It swims in warm seas.

Sand tiger shark
It might look as if a shark's nose would get in the way when it bites, but sharks can lift up their snouts, making their bite even stronger.

Winghead shark's head
The winghead is one of the hammerhead sharks. The wide, flat shape of its head helps it swim more efficiently.

Strange sharks

Some sharks look quite odd. They may resemble an old piece of carpet or a rough cloth. They may not look like sharks at all. Some have very strangely shaped heads. Others act in unusual ways.

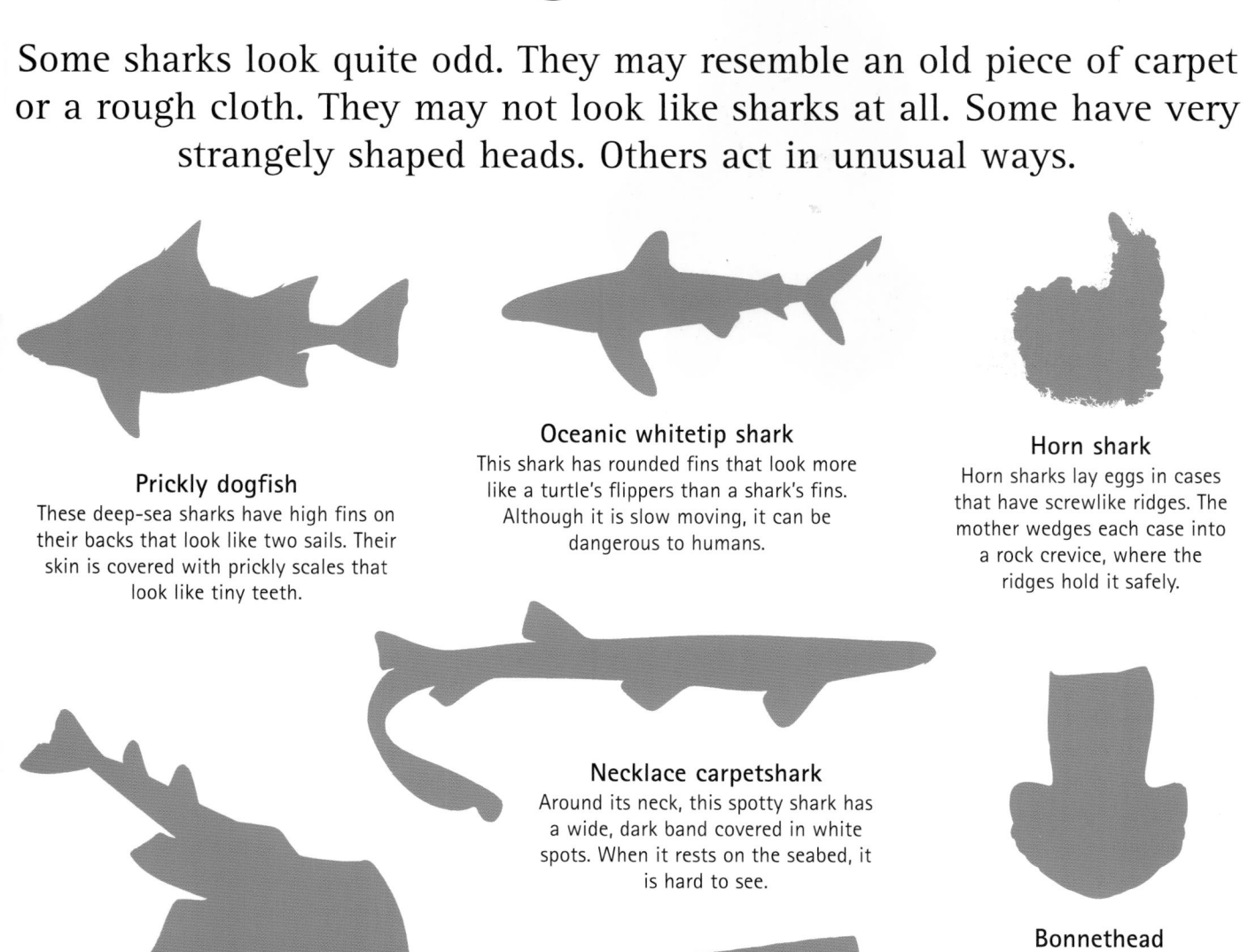

Prickly dogfish
These deep-sea sharks have high fins on their backs that look like two sails. Their skin is covered with prickly scales that look like tiny teeth.

Oceanic whitetip shark
This shark has rounded fins that look more like a turtle's flippers than a shark's fins. Although it is slow moving, it can be dangerous to humans.

Horn shark
Horn sharks lay eggs in cases that have screwlike ridges. The mother wedges each case into a rock crevice, where the ridges hold it safely.

Necklace carpetshark
Around its neck, this spotty shark has a wide, dark band covered in white spots. When it rests on the seabed, it is hard to see.

Angel shark
These sharks look a bit like rays. They bury themselves in the sandy seabed, and wait to ambush passing fish.

Frilled shark snout
The frilled shark looks more like an eel than a shark. It is named for the frills around its gills.

Bonnethead shark's head
The bonnethead shark has a smooth, shovel-shaped head.

Goblin shark
One of the most mysterious and bizarre sharks, this has a light pink, long, thin body, a pointy snout, and very, very long pointy teeth.

Tasseled wobbegong
These wobbegongs are patterned like a carpet and have little tassels hanging down over their mouth. They use their small, sharp teeth for crushing shellfish.

Shark food

Some sharks chase other sea creatures, hoping to catch them for food.
Others lie in wait, then pounce on animals that come near them.
Some eat the scraps from other animals' meals.

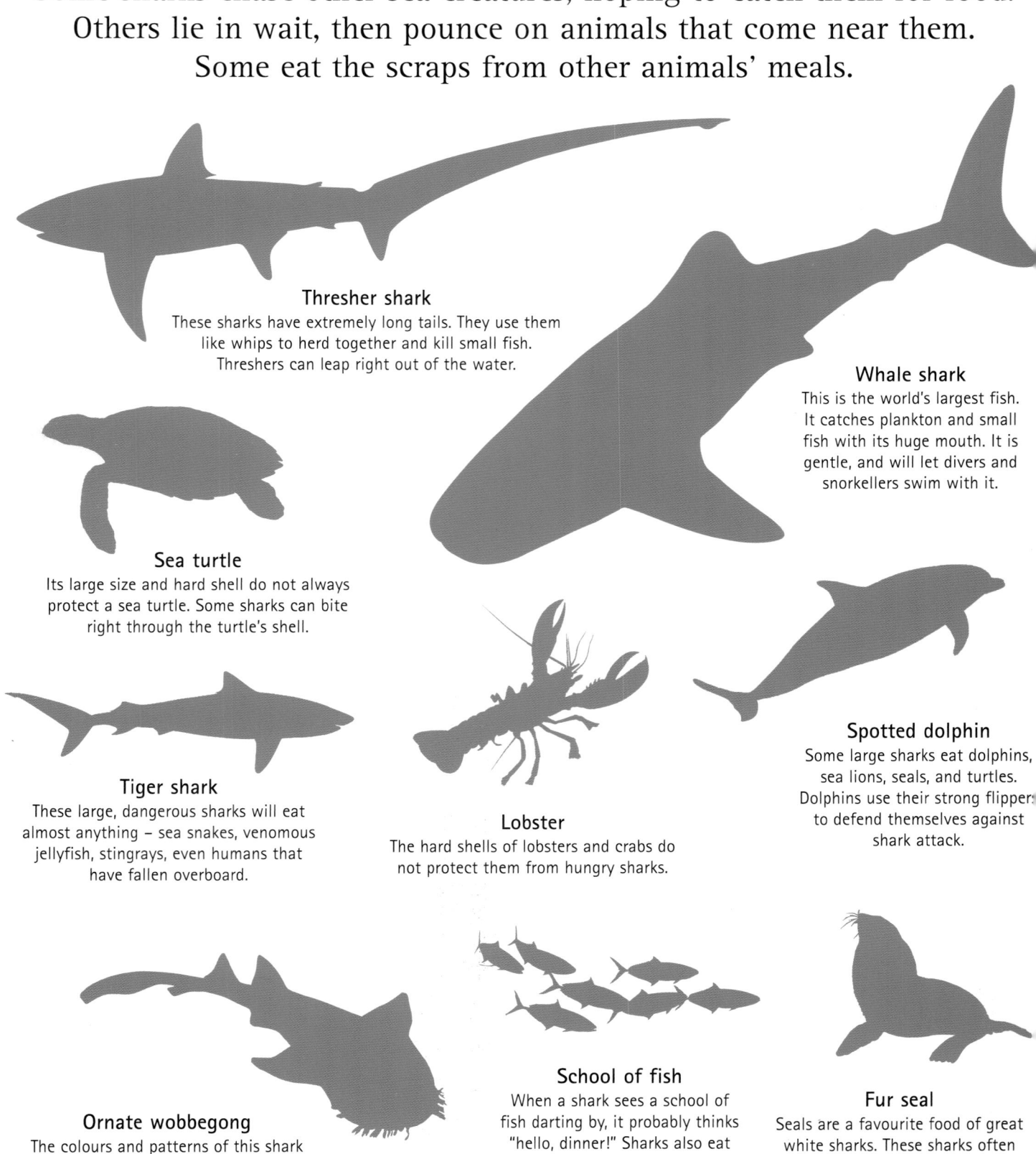

Thresher shark
These sharks have extremely long tails. They use them like whips to herd together and kill small fish. Threshers can leap right out of the water.

Whale shark
This is the world's largest fish. It catches plankton and small fish with its huge mouth. It is gentle, and will let divers and snorkellers swim with it.

Sea turtle
Its large size and hard shell do not always protect a sea turtle. Some sharks can bite right through the turtle's shell.

Spotted dolphin
Some large sharks eat dolphins, sea lions, seals, and turtles. Dolphins use their strong flippers to defend themselves against shark attack.

Tiger shark
These large, dangerous sharks will eat almost anything – sea snakes, venomous jellyfish, stingrays, even humans that have fallen overboard.

Lobster
The hard shells of lobsters and crabs do not protect them from hungry sharks.

Ornate wobbegong
The colours and patterns of this shark help it hide on the seafloor. It eats fish, octopus, crabs, and lobsters.

School of fish
When a shark sees a school of fish darting by, it probably thinks "hello, dinner!" Sharks also eat squid, sea urchins, crabs, worms, and sea birds.

Fur seal
Seals are a favourite food of great white sharks. These sharks often gather in places where seals and sea lions breed.